First Edition August, 1962

Library of Congress Card Number 62-19883

Published simultaneously in Canada by
Burns and MacEachern

Printed in the United States of America

PREFACE by David Lawrence

At last, in American history, a sad chapter of seeming ingratitude has been superseded by an act of gratitude. Congress now has passed a resolution tendering to General Douglas MacArthur the thanks of the nation for his distinguished military service to the American people.

So far as the official record is concerned, General MacArthur has been listed since 1951 as an officer removed from all command for alleged insubordination.

It happened that General MacArthur answered a letter of inquiry from the Republican leader in the House of Representatives, Joseph W. Martin of Massachusetts, who had asked the General for his opinion on Far Eastern questions. Military officers can testify freely before Congressional committees as long as they do not disclose military secrets. Yet a letter, which amounted to the same thing as testimony on broad policy problems, prompted the punishment that was meted out. The letter was never intended for publication.

General MacArthur had two commands at the time. He was commander of the Allied Occupation of Japan, and to this day it is universally agreed he did a wonderful job. He was also commander of the United Nations Forces in Korea. Had the American President wished, he could have changed commanders in Korea without disturbing the position of command which General MacArthur held in Japan. Mr. Truman was urged to do so by his own military chiefs in Washington and by some of his Cabinet officers but apparently chose to strip General MacArthur of all command and bring him home with a public repudiation.

For eleven years now the distinguished general has lived in retirement. Many of the men who served under him have not forgotten his remarkable acts of personal bravery and skillful command, and have felt that the nation should be reminded in a formal way of those contributions. It has been a delicate subject to raise. Finally a resolution before Congress passed unanimously. The resolution reads as follows:

"Resolved by the House of Representatives, the Senate concurring, that the thanks and appreciation of the Congress and the American people are hereby tendered to General of the Army Douglas MacArthur in recognition of his outstanding devotion to the American people, his brilliant leadership during and following World War II, and the unsurpassed affection held for him by the people of the Republic of the Philippines which has done so much to strengthen the ties of friendship between the people of that nation and the people of the United States."

What he did in liberating the Philippines from the Japanese in 1945, together with his remarkable service in the Korean War, are events recent enough for most people in this country to recall.

It does seem unfortunate, however, that a political incident has caused such a long delay in giving full recognition to a brave man who performed a brilliant service for his country in many command posts. At last the record has been set straight, and, fortunately, this comes during the lifetime of the 82-year-old veteran, who said in his farewell address to Congress in 1951: "Old soldiers never die—they just fade away."

Congress apparently is not willing that in official history the memory of what Douglas MacArthur did for his country should fade away but wants it to remain instead an enduring example of devotion to the nation's service.

Acknowledgement is made to David Lawrence, famous writer, and the New York Herald Tribune for their cooperation with this preface.

INTRODUCTION

On April 19, 1951, at Eniwetok, our atomic testing station in the Pacific, with a dozen or so Army, Navy and Air Force generals and admirals, and a sprinkling of civilian scientists, I listened to a radio broadcast of the address delivered by General of the Army Douglas MacArthur at Washington, D. C., before a joint meeting of the two houses of Congress in the hall of the House of Representatives.

I had seen MacArthur hold audiences spellbound before and this was no exception. As always, his profound knowledge of his subject, his clarity of presentation and his undoubted sincerity, held the attention of the listener to the end. When it was over you had the feeling that everyone took a deep breath, that they had forgotten to breathe as they didn't want to miss any of his words.

That day the members of Congress and the nation heard an expert analysis of the situation in the Far East, the story of Korea and some advice for the future that was good then and is still good today. The establishment in Japan of a representative, orderly and stable government, the recovery and the present prosperity of that country following a disastrous defeat, are primarily due to the wise and efficient administration of MacArthur, as Supreme Commander of the Allied Powers of Occupation. Never before in history has the Commander of an occupying army become a hero to the conquered people and never before has that army been as popular as the American soldiers, sailors and airmen have been in Japan. It was quite significant that when he needed them in Korea, MacArthur sent all four of the occupation divisions in Japan to the fighting front with no worry as to the effect of the resulting power vacuum in the Japanese who supported us through defeat, victory and the final inevitable stalemate that resulted from our policy which forbade operations against the main enemy, Red China, unless they were actually on Korean soil. As a result, Korea, the country we were trying to save, was bombed, shelled and devastated, while the real enemy, Red China, had its soil untouched.

Like all great leaders, MacArthur has his critics, some of whom have called him a warmonger, which is completely at variance with the facts. He has known war at first hand as few men have known it but he has long advocated its abolition as a means of settling international disputes. If, however, war is forced upon us, he believes that every means should be used to bring it to a swift, victorious end. He has never been a councilor of appeasement or surrender. History has always shown that such measures do not work. They result in a sham peace at best which merely lays the basis for more and more blackmail until violence is the only thing left. He is a realist who believes that under present world conditions we must maintain sufficient armed strength to deter any aggressor from attacking us and to win in case we are forced into war. In such an eventuality, as MacArthur has stated many times, "In war, there can be no substitute for victory."

He is a firm advocate of the first and most primary principle of war as well as statesmanship — that a great nation which voluntarily enters upon war and does not see it entirely to victory, will ultimately suffer all the consequences of defeat. He believes that our present jeopardizing conduct in the Far East is a direct result of our failure to follow through in the Korean conflict and that a no win policy always spells exactly what the words imply — defeat.

GENERAL GEORGE C. KENNEY

Address by

GENERAL OF THE ARMY
DOUGLAS MacARTHUR

before

a joint meeting of the
two houses of Congress in the
Hall of the House of Representatives
April 19, 1951

Mr. President, Mr. Speaker, and distinguished Members of the Congress:

I STAND on this rostrum with a sense of deep humility and great pride — humility in the wake of those great American architects of our history who have stood here before me, pride in the reflection that this forum of legislative debate represents human liberty in the purest form yet devised. Here are centered the hopes and aspirations and faith of the entire human race.

I do not stand here as advocate for any partisan cause, for the issues are fundamental and reach quite beyond the realm of partisan consideration. They must be resolved on the highest plane of national interest if our course is to prove sound and our future protected. I trust, therefore, that you will do me the justice of receiving that which I have to say as solely expressing the considered viewpoint of a fellow American. I address you with neither rancor nor bitterness in the fading twilight of life with but one purpose in mind — to serve my country.

The issues are global and so interlocked that to consider the problems of one sector, oblivious to those of another, is but to court disaster for the whole.

While Asia is commonly referred to as the gateway to Europe, it is no less true that Europe is the gateway to Asia, and the broad influence of the one cannot fail to have its impact upon the other.

There are those who claim our strength is inadequate to protect on both fronts — that we cannot divide our effort. I can think of no greater expression of defeatism. If a potential enemy can divide his strength on two fronts, it is for us to counter his effort.

[9]

The Communist threat is a global one. Its successful advance in one sector threatens the destruction of every other sector. You cannot appease or otherwise surrender to communism in Asia without simultaneously undermining our efforts to halt its advance in Europe.

Beyond pointing out these simple truisms, I shall confine my discussion to the general areas of Asia. Before one may objectively assess the situation now existing there, he must comprehend something of Asia's past and the revolutionary changes which have marked her course up to the present. Long exploited by the so-called colonial powers, with little opportunity to achieve any degree of social justice, individual dignity, or a higher standard of life such as guided our own noble administration of the Philippines, the peoples of Asia found their opportunity in the war just past to throw off the shackles of colonialism and now see the dawn of new opportunity, a heretofore unfelt dignity and the self-respect of political freedom.

Mustering half of the earth's population and 60 percent of its natural resources, these peoples are rapidly consolidating a new force, both moral and material, with which to raise the living standard and erect adaptations of the design of modern progress to their own distinct cultural environments. Whether one adheres to the concept of colonization or not, this is the direction of Asian progress and it may not be stopped. It is a corollary to the shift of the world economic frontiers, as the whole epicenter of world affairs rotates back toward the area whence it started. In this situation it becomes vital that our own country orient its policies in consonance with this basic evolutionary condition rather than pursue a course blind to the reality that the colonial era is now past and the Asian peoples covet the right to shape their own free destiny. What they seek now is friendly guidance, understanding, and support, not imperious direction; the dignity of equality, not the shame of subjugation. Their prewar standard of life, pitifully low, is infinitely lower now in the devastation left in war's wake. World ideologies play little part in Asian thinking and are little understood. What the peoples strive for is the opportunity for a little more food in their stomachs, a little better clothing on their backs, a little firmer roof over their heads, and the realization of the normal nationalist urge for political freedom. These political-social conditions have but an indirect bearing upon our own national security, but form a backdrop to contemporary planning which must be thoughtfully considered if we are to avoid the pitfalls of unrealism.

Of more direct and immediate bearing upon our national security are the changes wrought in the strategic potential of the Pacific Ocean in the course of the past war. Prior thereto, the western strategic frontier of the United States lay on the littoral line of the Americas with an exposed island salient extending out through Hawaii, Midway, and Guam to the Philippines. That salient proved not an outpost of strength but an avenue of weakness along which the enemy could and did attack. The Pacific was a potential area of advance for any predatory force intent upon striking at the bordering land areas.

All this was changed by our Pacific victory. Our strategic frontier then shifted to embrace the entire Pacific Ocean which became a vast moat to protect us as long as we hold it. Indeed, it acts as a protective shield for all of the Americas and all free lands of the Pacific Ocean area. We control it to the shores of Asia by a chain of islands extending in an arc from the Aleutians to the Mariannas held by us and our free allies. From this island chain we can dominate with sea and air power every Asiatic port from Vladivostok to Singapore and prevent any hostile movement into the Pacific. Any predatory attack from Asia must be an amphibious effort. No amphibious force can be successful without control of the sea lanes and the air over those lanes in its avenue of advance. With naval and air supremacy and modest ground elements to defend bases, any major attack from continental Asia toward us or our friends of the Pacific would be doomed to failure. Under such conditions the Pacific no longer represents menacing avenues of approach for a prospective invader — it assumes instead the friendly aspect of a peaceful lake. Our line of defense is a natural one and can be maintained with a minimum of military effort and expense. It envisions no attack against anyone nor does it provide the bastions essential for offensive operations, but properly maintained would be an invincible defense against aggression.

The holding of this littoral defense line in the western Pacific is entirely dependent upon holding all segments thereof, for any major breach of that line by an unfriendly power would render vulnerable to determined attack every other major segment. This is a military estimate as to which I have yet to find a military leader who will take exception. For that reason I have strongly recommended in the past as a matter of military urgency that under no circumstances must Formosa fall under Communist control. Such an eventuality would at once threaten the freedom of the Philippines and the loss of Japan, and might well force our Western frontier back to the coasts of California, Oregon, and Washington.

To understand the changes which now appear upon the Chinese mainland, one must understand the changes in Chinese character and culture over the past 50 years. China up to 50 years ago was completely nonhomogeneous, being compartmented into groups divided against each other. The war-making tendency was almost nonexistent, as they still followed the tenets of the Confucian ideal of pacifist culture. At the turn of the century, under the regime of Chan So Lin, efforts toward greater homogeneity produced the start of a nationalist urge. This was further and more successfully developed under the leadership of Chiang Kai-shek, but has been brought to its greatest fruition under the present regime, to the point that it has now taken on the character of a united nationalism of increasingly dominant aggressive tendencies. Through these past 50 years, the Chinese people have thus become militarized in their concepts and in their ideals. They now constitute excellent soldiers with competent staffs and commanders. This has produced a new and dominant power in Asia which for its own purposes is allied with Soviet Russia, but which in its own concepts and methods has become aggressively imperialistic with a lust for expansion and increased power normal to this type of imperialism. There is little of the ideological concept either one way or another in the Chinese make-up. The standard of living is so low and the capital accumulation has been so thoroughly dissipated by war that the masses are desperate and avid to follow any leadership which seems to promise the alleviation of local stringencies. I have from the beginning believed that the Chinese Communists' support of the North Koreans was the dominant one. Their interests are at present parallel to those of the Soviet, but I believe that the aggressiveness recently displayed not only in Korea, but also in Indochina and Tibet, and pointing potentially toward the south reflects predominantly the same lust for the expansion of power which has animated every would-be conqueror since the beginning of time.

The Japanese people since the war have undergone the greatest reformation recorded in modern history. With a commendable will, eagerness to learn, and marked capacity to understand, they have, from the ashes left in war's wake, erected in Japan an edifice dedicated to the primacy of individual liberty and personal dignity, and in the ensuing process there has been created a truly representative government committed to the advance of political morality, freedom of economic enterprise, and social justice. Politically, economically and socially Japan is now abreast of many free nations of the earth and will not again fail the universal trust. That it may be counted upon to wield a profoundly beneficial influence over the course of events in Asia is attested by the magnificent manner in which the Japanese people have met the recent challenge of war, unrest and confusion surrounding them from the outside, and checked communism within their own frontiers without the slightest slackening in their forward progress. I sent all four of our occupation divisions to the Korean battle front without the slightest qualms as to the effect of the resulting power vacuum upon Japan. The results fully justified my faith. I know of no nation more serene, orderly and industrious — nor in which higher hopes can be entertained for future constructive service in the advance of the human race.

Of our former ward, the Philippines, we can look forward in confidence that the existing unrest will be corrected and a strong and healthy nation will grow in the longer aftermath of war's terrible destructiveness. We must be patient and understanding and never fail them, as in our hour of need they did not fail us. A Christian nation, the Philippines stand as a mighty bulwark of Christianity in the Far East, and its capacity for high moral leadership in Asia is unlimited.

On Formosa, the Government of the Republic of China has had the opportunity to refute by action much of the malicious gossip which so undermined the strength of its leadership on the Chinese mainland. The Formosan people are receiving a just and enlightened administration with majority representation on the organs of government, and politically, economically and socially they appear to be advancing along sound and constructive lines.

With this brief insight into the surrounding areas I now turn to the Korean conflict. While I was not consulted prior to the President's decision to intervene in support of the Republic of Korea, that decision, from a military standpoint, proved a sound one, as we hurled back the invader and decimated his forces. Our victory was complete and our objectives within reach when Red China intervened with numerically superior ground forces. This created a new war and an entirely new situation — a situation not contemplated when our forces were committed against the North Korean invaders — a situation which called for new decisions in the diplomatic sphere to permit the realistic adjustment of military strategy. Such decisions have not been forthcoming.

While no man in his right mind would advocate sending our ground forces into continental China and such was never given a thought, the new situation did urgently demand a drastic revision of strategic planning if our political aim was to defeat this new enemy as we had defeated the old.

Apart from the military need as I saw it to neutralize the sanctuary protection given the enemy north of the Yalu, I felt that military necessity in the conduct of the war made mandatory:

1. The intensification of our economic blockade against China;

There are some who for varying reasons would appease Red China. They are blind to history's clear lesson. For history teaches with unmistakable emphasis that appeasement but begets new and bloodier war. It points to no single instance where the end has justified that means — where appeasement has led to more than a sham peace. Like blackmail, it lays the basis for new and successively greater demands, until, as in blackmail, violence becomes the only alternative. Why, my soldiers asked of me, surrender military advantages to an enemy in the field? I could not answer. Some may say to avoid spread of the conflict into an all-out war with China; others, to avoid Soviet intervention. Neither explanation seems valid. For China is already engaging with the maximum power it can commit and the Soviet will not necessarily mesh its actions with our moves. Like a cobra, any new enemy will more likely strike whenever it feels that the relativity in military or other potential is in its favor on a world-wide basis.

The tragedy of Korea is further heightened by the fact that as military action is confined to its territorial limits, it condemns that nation, which it is our purpose to save, to suffer the devastating impact of full naval and air bombardment, while the enemy's sanctuaries are fully protected from such attack and devastation. Of the nations of the world, Korea alone, up to now, is the sole one which has risked its all against communism. The magnificence of the courage and fortitude of the Korean people defies description. They have chosen to risk death rather than slavery. Their last words to me were "Don't scuttle the Pacific."

I have just left your fighting sons in Korea. They have met all tests there and I can report to you without reservation they are splendid in every way. It was my constant effort to preserve them and end this savage conflict honorably and with the least loss of time and a minimum sacrifice of life. Its growing bloodshed has caused me the deepest anguish and anxiety. Those gallant men will remain often in my thoughts and in my prayers always.

I am closing my 52 years of military service. When I joined the Army even before the turn of the century, it was the fulfillment of all my boyish hopes and dreams. The world has turned over many times since I took the oath on the Plain at West Point, and the hopes and dreams have long since vanished. But I still remember the refrain of one of the most popular barrack ballads of that day which proclaimed most proudly that —

"Old soldiers never die; they just fade away."

And like the old soldier of that ballad, I now close my military career and just fade away — an old soldier who tried to do his duty as God gave him the light to see that duty.

Good-by.

INTRODUCTION

General James A. Van Fleet wanted to write the intro-duction to Duty-Honor-Country, as indicated on the front of the jacket of this book, but at the moment Van Fleet is in Korea and not within reach; his introduction will be de-layed until the second edition. Meanwhile, Douglas Mac-Arthur's "official portrait painter" in both world wars is chosen as the substitute.

We all know General of the Army Douglas MacArthur well. We were of the millions who gave this General the greatest welcome home any man ever received. All hearts were pounding! His complete success as the Supreme Com-mander in the Pacific area is history for the world and will endure to the end of time.

While painting portraits for the Government with the American Expeditionary Forces in World War I, I found the young commander of the 42nd (Rainbow) Division at Sinzig. In fact, he was the youngest commander of them all and was a very busy man. I saw wound stripes on his sleeve. He had been awarded the Distinguished Service Cross and had been given the threat that if he did not keep away from the front line of battle he would be sent home. The idea behind the threat, of course, was that it takes too long to make a General to have his life sacrificed at the front. How-ever, Duty-Honor-Country was foremost in his mind, and needless to say, he was "at the front" more than he was not.

As great men always are, he was gracious, understanding, considerate. When he discovered I had no billet, he set a cot up for me near his own, saying it was *my* billet to use whenever I needed it.

In World War II, probably no man knew another man so thoroughly as General Wainright knew MacArthur. While painting the portrait of that suffering General, I listened to his words. The broken voice said of MacArthur: "I'd follow that man — anywhere — blindfolded." My heart missed a beat; I could hear Sousa's band playing *The Stars and Stripes Forever.*

We know of attempts to discredit MacArthur, but we also know he cannot be discredited and our Country is proud. Today Congress is not agreeable that in the official records of history the memory of General of the Army Douglas MacArthur's accomplishments should go unheeded, but that what does remain will be the thanks of a nation to a great General whose life was spent in devotion to his country. *His* motto truly is, Duty-Honor-Country.

JOSEPH CUMMINGS CHASE

Address by

GENERAL OF THE ARMY
DOUGLAS MACARTHUR

to

The Members of the Association of Graduates, U.S.M.A.

The Corps of Cadets and Distinguished Guests

upon his acceptance of

THE SYLVANUS THAYER AWARD

United States Military Academy, West Point, New York

May 12, 1962

General Westmoreland, General Groves, distinguished guests, and gentlemen of the Corps:

As I was leaving the hotel this morning, a doorman asked me, "Where are you bound for, General?" and when I replied, "West Point," he remarked, "Beautiful place, have you ever been there before?"

No human being could fail to be deeply moved by such a tribute as this. [Thayer Award] Coming from a profession I have served so long, and a people I have loved so well, it fills me with an emotion I cannot express. But this award is not intended primarily to honor a personality, but to symbolize a great moral code — the code of conduct and chivalry of those who guard this beloved land of culture and ancient descent. That is the meaning of this medallion. For all eyes and for all time, it is an expression of the ethics of the American soldier. That I should be integrated in this way with so noble an ideal arouses a sense of pride and yet of humility which will be with me always.

Duty — Honor — Country. Those three hallowed words reverently dictate what you ought to be, what you can be, what you will be. They are your rallying points: to build courage when courage seems to fail; to regain faith when there seems to be little cause for faith; to create hope when hope becomes forlorn. Unhappily, I possess neither that eloquence of diction, that poetry of imagination, nor that brilliance of metaphor to tell you all that they mean. The unbelievers will say they are but words, but a slogan, but a flamboyant phrase. Every pedant, every demagogue, every cynic, every hypocrite, every troublemaker, and, I am sorry to say, some others of an entirely different character, will try to downgrade them even to the extent of mockery and ridicule. But these are some of the things they do. They build your basic character, they mold you for your future roles as custodians of the nation's defense, they make you strong enough to know when you are weak, and brave enough to face yourself when you are afraid. They teach you to be proud and unbending in honest failure, but humble and gentle in success; not to substitute words for actions, nor to seek the path of comfort, but to face the stress and spur of difficulty and challenge; to learn to stand up in the storm but to have compassion on those who fall; to master yourself before you seek to master others; to have a heart that is clean, a goal that is high; to learn to laugh yet never forget how to weep; to reach into the future yet never neglect the past; to be serious yet never to take yourself too seriously; to be modest so that you will remember the simplicity of true greatness, the open mind of true wisdom, the meekness of true strength. They give you a temper of the will, a quality of the imagination, a vigor of the emotions, a freshness of the deep springs of life, a temperamental predominance of courage over timidity, an appetite for adventure over love of ease. They create in your heart the sense of wonder, the unfailing hope of what next, and the joy and inspiration of life. They teach you in this way to be an officer and a gentleman.

And what sort of soldiers are those you are to lead? Are they reliable, are they brave, are they capable of victory? Their story is known to all of you; it is the story of the American man-at-arms. My estimate of him was formed on the battlefield many, many years ago, and has never changed. I regarded him then as I regard him now — as one of the world's noblest figures, not only as one of the finest military characters but also as one of the most stainless. His name and fame are the birthright of every American citizen. In his youth and strength, his love and loyalty he gave — all that mortality can give. He needs no eulogy from me or from any other man. He has written his own history and written it in red on his enemy's breast. But when I think of his patience under adversity, of his courage under fire, and of his modesty in victory, I am filled with an emotion of admiration I cannot put into words. He belongs to history as furnishing one of the greatest examples of successful patriotism; he belongs to posterity as the instructor of future generations in the principles of liberty and freedom; he belongs to the present, to us, by his virtues and by his achievements. In 20 campaigns, on a hundred battlefields, around a thousand campfires, I have witnessed that enduring fortitude, that patriotic self-abnegation, and that invincible determination which have carved his statue in the hearts of his people. From one end of the world to the other he has drained deep the chalice of courage.

As I listened to those songs of the glee club, in memory's eye I could see those staggering columns of the First World War, bending under soggy packs, on many a weary march from dripping dusk to drizzling dawn, slogging ankle-deep through the mire of shell-shocked roads, to form grimly for the attack, blue-lipped, covered with sludge and mud, chilled by the wind and rain; driving home to their objective, and, for many, to the judgment seat of God. I do not know the dignity of their birth but I do know the glory of their death. They died unquestioning, uncomplaining, with faith in their hearts, and on their lips the hope that we would go on to victory. Always for them — Duty — Honor — Country; always their blood and sweat and tears as we sought the way and the light and the truth.

And 20 years after, on the other side of the globe, again the filth of murky foxholes, the stench of ghostly trenches, the slime of dripping dugouts; those boiling suns of relentless heat, those torrential rains of devastating storms; the loneliness and utter desolation of jungle trails, the bitterness of long separation from those they loved and cherished, the deadly pestilence of tropical disease, the horror of stricken areas of war; their resolute and determined defense, their swift and sure attack, their indomitable purpose, their complete and decisive victory — always victory. Always through the bloody haze of their last reverberating shot, the vision of gaunt, ghastly men reverently following your password of Duty — Honor — Country.

The code which those words perpetuate embraces the highest moral laws and will stand the test of any ethics or philosophies ever promulgated for the uplift of mankind. Its requirements are for the things that are right, and its restraints are from the things that are wrong. The soldier, above all other men, is required to practice the greatest act of religious training — sacrifice. In battle and in the face of danger and death, he discloses those divine attributes which his Maker gave when he created man in his own image. No physical courage and no brute instinct can take the place of the Divine help which alone can sustain him. However horrible the incidents of war may be, the soldier who is called upon to offer and to give his life for his country is the noblest development of mankind.

You now face a new world — a world of change. The thrust into outer space of the satelites, spheres and missiles marked the beginning of another epoch in the long story of mankind — the chapter of the space age. In the five or more billions of years the scientists tell us it has taken to form the earth, in the three or more billion years of development of the human race, there has never been a greater, a more abrupt or staggering evolution. We deal now not with things of this world alone, but with the illimitable distances and as yet unfathomed mysteries of the universe. We are reaching out for a new and boundless frontier. We speak in strange terms: of harnessing the cosmic energy; of making winds and tides work for us; of creating unheard of synthetic materials to supplement or even replace our old standard basics; of purifying sea water for our drink; of mining ocean floors for new fields of wealth and food; of disease preventatives to expand life into the hundreds of years; of controlling the weather for a more equitable distribution of heat and cold, of rain and shine; of space ships to the moon; of the primary target in war, no longer limited to the armed forces of an enemy, but instead to include his civil populations; of ultimate conflict between a united human race and the sinister forces of some other planetary galaxy; of such dreams and fantasies as to make life the most exciting of all time.

And through all this welter of change and development, your mission remains fixed, determined, inviolable — it is to win our wars. Everything else in your professional career is but a corollary to this vital dedication. All other public purposes, all other public projects, all other public needs, great or small, will find others for their accomplishment; but you are the ones who are trained to fight: yours is the profession of arms — the will to win, the sure knowledge that in war there is no substitute for victory; that if you lose, the nation will be destroyed; that the very obsession of your public service must be Duty — Honor — Country. Others will debate the controversial issues, national and international, which divide men's minds; but serene, calm, aloof, you stand as the nation's war-guardian, as its lifeguard from the raging tides of international conflict, as its gladiator in the arena of battle. For a century and a half you have defended, guarded, and protected its hallowed traditions of liberty and freedom, of right and justice. Let civilian voices argue the merits or demerits of our processes of government; whether our strength is being sapped by deficit financing, indulged in too long, by federal paternalism grown too mighty, by power groups grown too arrogant, by politics grown too corrupt, by crime grown too rampant, by morals grown too low, by taxes grown too high, by extremists grown too violent; whether our personal liberties are as thorough and complete as they should be. These great national problems are not for your professional participation or military solution. Your guidepost stands out like a ten-fold beacon in the night — Duty — Honor — Country.

You are the leaven which binds together the entire fabric of our national system of defense. From your ranks come the great captains who hold the nation's destiny in their hands the moment the war tocsin sounds. The Long Gray Line has never failed us. Were you to do so, a million ghosts in olive drab, in brown khaki, in blue and gray, would rise from their white crosses thundering those magic words — Duty — Honor — Country.

This does not mean that you are war mongers. On the contrary, the soldier, above all other people, prays for peace, for he must suffer and bear the deepest wounds and scars of war. But always in our ears ring the ominous words of Plato, that wisest of all philosophers, "Only the dead have seen the end of war."

The shadows are lengthening for me. The twilight is here. My days of old have vanished tone and tint; they have gone glimmering through the dream of things that were. Their memory is one of wondrous beauty, watered by tears, and coaxed and caressed by the smiles of yesterday. I listen vainly for the witching melody of faint bugles blowing reveille, of far drums beating the long roll. In my dreams I hear again the crash of guns, the rattle of musketry, the strange, mournful mutter of the battlefield.

But in the evening of my memory, always I come back to West Point. Always there echoes and re-echoes — Duty — Honor — Country.

Today marks my final roll call with you, but I want you to know that when I cross the river my last conscious thoughts will be of The Corps, and The Corps, and The Corps.

I bid you farewell.